An Evening Dream in Springtime:
Memories of My Grandfather

An Evening Dream in Springtime

Memories of My Grandfather

Written by *Mika Matsuno* | Illustrated by *Jack Lefcourt*

BELLE ISLE BOOKS
www.belleislebooks.com

ISBN: 978-1-951565-62-6
LCCN: 2020917974

Cover and layout design by Michael Hardison
Production management by Tanya Pruett

Printed in the United States of America

Published by
Belle Isle Books (an imprint of Brandylane Publishers, Inc.)
5 S. 1st Street
Richmond, Virginia 23219

BELLE ISLE BOOKS
www.belleislebooks.com

belleislebooks.com | brandylanepublishers.com

*This book is dedicated to
my parents; my sister; my aunts and uncles;
my grandparents and their forebears;
as well as to the hardworking staff
at my grandfather's restaurant, two skillful chefs
named Hosoda-san and Baba-chan, who have been
like a part of my family for so many years.
But most of all, this book is dedicated to
my paternal grandfather, Matsujiro,
whose spirit still resides in Kyoto,
in the city where I was born.*

Grandparents are not easy to know.
They come from different worlds than we do.
And yet, we are connected.

My grandfather has two names. Originally, he was named Matsujiro (松二郎) and in the middle of his life, changed his name to Keisuke (圭祐). His family name is Matsuno (松野), so his full name is Matsuno Matsujiro (松野 松二郎). Both his family name and his given name, Matsujiro, have the same *kanji* (松). This *kanji* symbol means "pine tree." Perhaps it gave his full name a slightly unsophisticated sound. In my imperfect memory, someone told me that was why he changed his name. Or maybe I just believe so.

My father was named Keiichi (圭一), taking the *kanji* character 圭 from my grandfather's name. My older sister was named Keiko (圭子), also taking 圭 from my grandfather's. Their names both took the *kanji* 圭 from my grandfather's, but mine didn't. This was a hurtful point for me when I was a child. My own name, Mika (美香), did not carry his name, and yet, some say I was closest to him.

3

My grandfather couldn't walk without sticks because of polio he suffered from as a child. His leg joints were stiff, so even using his sticks, walking was hard. He often grimaced with pain.

Together, he and my grandmother, whose name was Mine (pronounced "ME-nay," みね), ran a traditional Japanese food restaurant on Shichijo Street. This restaurant, Minori, was in our family for nearly one hundred years. I sometimes helped in the kitchen. It wasn't easy work.

Most Saturday nights, I would stay at my grandparents' house. Since it was just a one-stop train ride from my home, it was near enough to go on foot. But with no sidewalk and few other pedestrians, the way there was not so enjoyable.

I had to walk under the railway overpass on the way, which I disliked very much. The passage was dank, colorless, and gloomy. The cracks in the walls were caked with something like plants. Strange liquid dropped from overhead and moistened the pavement.

The thought that the liquid might drop on my head or that I might be trapped there in that dark, dreadful place got me running. I ran most of the way to their house.

The Kamo-gawa, the river in Kyoto that moves slowly alongside Division Street, runs very near where my grandparents' house stood. Earth, sand, and junk that flowed from the headwaters accumulated there. I always walked quickly to get past that depressing sight and rushed right into their house.

When I opened the door, there Grandfather would be, practicing his calligraphy.

"I am here, Grandfather!" I'd call, and he would look up from his work and say, "Oh, hello, Mika-chan. It was sweet of you to come!" His smile was a welcome sight, and at those moments, it seemed to restore color to the world!

My grandfather used to wear a brightly-colored down vest and a colorful woolen cap to keep warm from the winter cold. He was a handsome man and looked good in them, but there was something funny and cute about my grandfather in his cap. "You look sweet in that cap!" I always felt like saying.

I would often spend time beside him, watching his careful brushstrokes. My grandfather never studied beyond elementary school, not uncommon in his time, but his handwriting was very elegant.

My grandfather studied *shodo* (Japanese calligraphy) on his own. I also studied *shodo* when I was an elementary school student. I went to an after-school class with brand-new calligraphy tools my parents bought for me. Some of my friends also joined in. Elementary school students in those days had few day-to-day opportunities to write *kanji* with a brush. Practicing calligraphy once a week in our after-school class was a treat! We were happy to experience these simple things: sitting on our heels, rubbing an India ink stick on a stone, and producing the ancient characters with a brush.

For my grandfather, it was more difficult. He had to help with his family's restaurant, even as a child, and his parents couldn't afford to give him *shodo* lessons. Even if he had been allowed to attend classes, he still would have had to clear some hurdles. In his shoes, I'm not sure I would have been able to sustain my enthusiasm to study *shodo*. I wonder what inspired him to become so talented.

My grandfather wrote *tanka* poems with a brush. *Tanka* is an ancient form of Japanese verse, consisting of five lines of 5, 7, 5, 7, and 7 syllables. He enjoyed copying verses from the *Manyo-shu*, the oldest existing anthology of classical Japanese poetry.

The collection includes eighth-century poems written by poets from all walks of life, from emperors to common people, but those by the Sakimori and their families stood out most to me. The Sakimori were ancient coast guards who had to walk on foot from eastern Japan to northern Kyushu to serve often years longer than their three-year terms.

Their poems speak of the arduous journey, their profound sadness at being sent so far from home, their wives' aches and hopes. As the poems were written in old Japanese, I could barely understand them. Yet printed on smooth paper in full color, the scenic pictures of their frontier landscapes gave me some sense of the Sakimori's loneliness, insecurity, and longing.

A black wooden writing box sat on my grandfather's desk, along with a metal paperweight and a writing carpet. The writing box contained brushes, an ink stone, an India ink stick, and a tiny water container. With these simple tools and some Japanese writing paper, an artist can do calligraphy.

Japanese calligraphy starts with pouring water onto an ink stone and then slowly rubbing an India ink stick on the stone. It takes time to prepare liquid ink this way.

These days, ready-made ink is available in large containers. However, it is said that the more traditional manner of rubbing the ink stick on the stone is very important. It helps one obtain serenity of mind and also gives shades to the ink, adding subtle charm to an artist's work.

The surface of the ceramic water container my grandfather used was white and very smooth, with a blue landscape depicted on it. It had a small hole through which the water was poured onto the stone. He had a small black hexahedron India ink stick called a *sumi*, with chrysanthemum flower designs carved on the surface in gold leaf.

Grandfather would spread a bit of water on an ink stone with a *sumi* and start rubbing them together slowly, with concentration. When rubbed against the stone, the scent of the *sumi* was crisp and tense. It always had a powerful effect on me. My back would straighten, and I would become calm. I prepared my own body and soul for doing *shodo* in this way.

書道

My grandfather stamped his name in red on all his works using a stone upon which he had carved his name. I think his best work was a Buddhist *sutra* written to form the shape of a pagoda. It was much bigger than any of his other pieces, combining his calligraphy and drawing. It was truly original. I had never seen anything like it. His signature stamp in red was, to my childhood mind, like a bold declaration: "This is me. Grandfather."

Although he didn't get special education, the work with Grandfather's stamp on it turned out to be compelling, distinguished works of art. Some people from overseas once came to my grandfather's house in Kyoto and asked to see some of his work. How did they hear about my grandfather? To my knowledge, he had never sold a piece or been picked up by the media. That memory still baffles me. Maybe in some faraway place, his works were revered? I'll never know and will always wonder.

Strange things were displayed in my grandfather's house. Only some of them I remember now. There used to be a horse-shaped metal sculpture, which was solid and heavy. Its surface was shiny. The horse stepped high as if it could take off running at any moment. It looked strong and heroic, maybe a bit fierce. I would sit for a long time staring at it.

My grandfather was born in the year of the horse, the "Hinoe Horse," it was called. The year of the Hinoe Horse comes once every sixty years. There is a superstition that women born in the year of the Hinoe Horse will kill their husbands.

Nobody takes that seriously, of course, but it is said that a person born in the year of the Hinoe Horse has a fiery temper. ". . . Because he was born in the year of the Hinoe Horse," someone might say.

But actually, my grandfather was always warm and gentle. I am proud of him. He supported his mother, wife, and children. Grandfather overcame adversity in difficult times. He must have been brave, strong, and tough, like a horse. I think he was a miracle.

A *Noh* mask and a doll were also displayed. The *Noh* mask hung on the wall, the woman's stony face in white makeup staring down at me with her scary eyes. I could never tell if she was smiling or wicked.

I think the doll was a *kabuki* actor playing the *shishi*, which is an imaginary creature based on a lion. I have seen a *kabuki* actor dressed like the doll performing *shishi* on TV. The *kabuki* actor was swinging his long, flowing red hair about like a lion's mane. To me it looked eccentric and crazy.

To be honest, I didn't appreciate my grandfather's taste for these scary things, and as a child, I could not understand why he had them on display. Why didn't I ask him then? Or did I, and just can't remember?

Sadly, his house doesn't exist anymore. It was destroyed under the land readjustment project in 2000. Only a few pictures of him and his writings remain to show he used to exist at all.

But I still remember my grandfather's voice! I recall the strange words he often used. He referred to himself as "*ate*," not *watashi*, *washi*, *boku*, or *ore*, and to his bottom as "*oido*," not *oshiri*. He usually said "thank you" as "*ookini*" instead of *arigato*.

Before dinner, Grandfather always chanted a Buddhist *sutra*, "*Nanmandabu, nanmandabu* (南無阿弥陀仏)," at our family altar, sitting on his heels. It sounded like a foreign song. I didn't understand the words he recited at all. His voice was resonant and stirring. It would gradually become louder and begin reverberating, and I was always overwhelmed by its power. Then it would soften, until finally he murmured so quietly that I could barely hear him at all.

Sometimes the melody was lost, and he seemed to speak to our ancestors, not in a Buddhist *sutra*, but in his own, made-up words. I could catch some of them. "Thank you. . ." he drawled, "*Nanmandabuuuuu* （南無阿弥陀仏）," and beat the small, cup-shaped gong with a small stick. Although hazy to me, this could be roughly translated as "Thank you, Amidabutsu" (Amidabutsu being one of several Buddhist names for God). The sounds of "u" and the gong lingered in the air like a thread of smoke.

As a child, I wondered why my grandfather, an amateur, could chant the *sutra* so well. He must have practiced in secret, or perhaps it became his gift after practicing daily for so many years?

Nearly twenty years later, at my grandfather's funeral, I heard a professional monk recite a *sutra*. It was not satisfactory to me. Something was missing! His performance was not as powerful as my grandfather's and lacked his unique inflection. While listening to the monk reciting, I said aloud that Grandfather was much better. Perhaps I should have refrained from doing so.

One day when I was a child, at his birthday or my grandparents' wedding anniversary—I am not certain—Grandfather performed a song for us. He sang very differently from other singers familiar to me. The room resounded with his voice!

Now that I think about it, the song may have been a passage from *The Tale of the Heike*. *The Tale of the Heike* is a story of war, the rise to glory and eventual downfall of the Heike clan. It is said to have been written in the thirteenth century, in the Kamakura period. It was sung

to the accompaniment of a *biwa*, a four- or five-stringed musical instrument similar to a lute. Blind monks, called *biwa hoshi* (or *biwa* players), walked all over Japan to sing and narrate *The Tale of the Heike*. It was welcomed as oral literature by many illiterate or common people. The story warns that the proud and prosperous do not endure and is based on the Buddhist concept of the impermanence of worldly things.

My grandfather used to take *Chikuzen biwa* lessons from a *biwa* master. The master gave him a stage name, Kyokkou (旭鴻). It is said that my grandfather used to have a gorgeous stage costume.

I learned of this more than ten years after he passed away. Despite him having a stage name and stage costume, even my own father never saw Grandfather sing or play the *biwa*. We can only imagine, in memory, in wonder.

Every year in April, the cherry blossoms spring to fullness, almost unbelievably—and then they are gone. Billowy clouds of pink and white rustle in the branches above and alongside streets and rivers, in parks, and on temple grounds. Like magic, they appear. And then, moments later it seems, the petals weaken and fall, and the wind takes them away.

I always thought I knew my grandfather. But really, all I know is just a little part of everything he was. His own sweet memories of childhood, and all his dreams that never came true, are gone. They are like an evening dream in springtime.

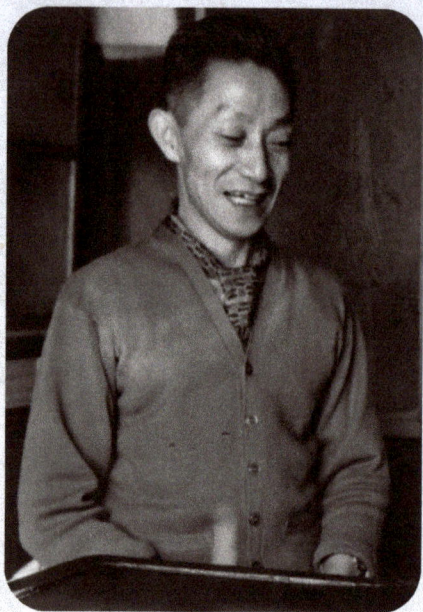

Matsuno Matsujiro

松野　松二郎

About the Author

Mika Matsuno was born in Kyoto, Japan, in 1965 and grew up in a house along Shichijo Street, a stone's throw from Kyoto's famed Kamo River. She spent much of her childhood helping out in her grandfather's restaurant, an old establishment called Minori, which thrived for several generations in her family until it closed for good in 2014. Through her grandfather, she also developed a talent for *shodo*, the traditional art of Japanese calligraphy. Mika attended Kyoto's Doshisha University, where she majored in psychology. After graduating in 1988, she went to work for a large Japanese electronics company for close to a decade. Weary of desk work, in 1997 Mika chose to do a bit of exploring and moved to Italy, living for a stretch in both Florence and Ravenna, where she studied the Italian language and developed a keen interest in local culinary and cultural traditions. Upon returning to Japan, she worked at various jobs while continuing her foreign language studies. For four years starting in 2007, Mika built and helped run a small English language school in Kyoto and subsequently taught basic Japanese to foreign workers at a vocational college. For the past thirty years, Mika has also practiced the ancient custom of tea ceremony, in the Urasenke tradition, a passion she pursues to this day.

About the Illustrator

Jack Lefcourt was born in Kitchener, just outside Toronto, Canada, in 1964. He earned a bachelor's degree in fine arts from the University of Waterloo in 1988. Jack's cartooning and illustration career spans several decades. His editorial work has appeared in some sixty newspapers and magazines across Canada. He is also a teacher, having earned his bachelor's of education from Brock University in Ontario and currently teaches English in Japan, where he has lived since 2006.

www.ingramcontent.com/pod-product-compliance
Lightning Source LLC
Chambersburg PA
CBHW051216150426
R18143100001BA/R181431PG42813CBX00008BA/3